Beth Israel Cemetery

The Grave Whisperer

Angeline Gallant

Published by Angeline Gallant, 2022.

BETH ISRAEL CEMETERY

First edition. November 14, 2022.

ISBN: 979-8215768952

Written by Angeline Gallant.

Also by Angeline Gallant

A Dragon's Diary
Dreaming of Dragons

Calling Her Heart
Whisper of the Heart
No Turning Back
Forsake Me Not
Hear My Cry
Calling Her Heart Boxed Set Volumes 1-4

FORGET ME NOT
Victoria, Ontario's Babies 1894 - 1895

Keeper Of Secrets
A Lady's Secret

Midnight's Awakening

Heart of the Storm
Walking Through The Storm
Midnight's Awakening boxed set volumes 1-3

Secrets of the Underworld
Deklan's Dragons
Secrets of the Underworld Volumes 1 & 2

Tell My Story Collection
Tell My Story: England 1852

The Grave Whisperer
Wedding Bells in Kingston, Ontario, Canada 1923
St. Paul's Anglican Churchyard Kingston, Ontario, Canada A-B
St. Paul's Anglican Churchyard, Kingston, Ontario, Canada C - D
St. Paul's Anglican Churchyard, Kingston, Ontario, Canada G - H
St. Paul's Anglican Churchyard, Kingston, Ontario, Canada J - N
St. Paul's Anglican Churchyard, Kingston, Ontario, Canada O - R
St. Paul's Anglican Churchyard, Kingston, Ontario, Canada S - T
St. Paul's Anglican Churchyard, Kingston, Ontario T - Z
Small Graveyards & Burial Grounds: Kingston, Ontario, Canada
Cataraqui United Church Cemetery 1
Cataraqui United Church Cemetery 2
Cataraqui United Church Cemetary 3
Cataraqui United Church Cemetery 4
Cataraqui United Church Cemetery 5
Beth Israel Cemetery

The Wolf Whisperer Series
The Cry of the Wolf
Captured Heart
Journey of the Heart
Fate's Legacy
Wolf Whisperer volumes 1 & 2
Endless White
The Wolf Whisperer Volumes 1-4

Standalone
Winds of Change vol 1-3

Watch for more at https://www.goodreads.com/author/show/
19703964.Angeline_Gallant.

Table of Contents

BETH ISRAEL CEMETERY IN KINGSTON, ONTARIO, CANADA

DORIS (KIZELL) BEROFE[1]

Doris was born in Killaloe, Renfrew, Ontario in October 1921. She was 12 years old when the Dionne Quintuplets were born in 1934.

Doris was 47 years old when her father passed away in 1969.

She was 60 years old when the Canada Act was passed in 1982.

Doris was 65 years old when her brother, Aaron, passed away in 1987.

She was 74 years old when she passed away on January 4, 1996.

HARRY BEROFE[2]

Harry was born on June 15, 1916.

He was 17 years old when the Dionne Quintuplets were born in 1934.

Harry was 65 years old when the Canada Act was passed in 1982.

He was 79 years old when his wife passed away in 1996.

Harry was 92 years old when he passed away on June 1, 2008.

BERYL RUTH COHEN[3]

Beryl was born on November 6, 1959.
She was 22 years old when the Canada Act was passed in 1892.
Beryl was 62 years old when she passed away on April 17, 2022.

ALFRED JOEL FISHER[4]

Alfred was born in 1942.

He was 40 years old when the Canada Act was passed in 1982. Alfred was 74 years old when he passed away in 2016.

SHARI BETH GINSBERG[5]

S hari was born in 1958.
　　She was 24 years old when the Canada Act was passed in 1982.
Shari was 56 years old when she passed away in 2014.

AARON GOLDSTEIN[6]

Aaron was born in 1936.
He was 46 years old when the Canada Act was passed in 1982.
He was 82 years old when he passed away on September 30, 2018.

GLORIA EVE GOLDSTEIN[7]

Gloria was born in 1960.

She was 22 years old when the Canada Act was passed in 1982. Gloria was 25 years old when she passed away in 1985.

DR. AUBREY GROLL[8]

Aubrey was born in 1934.

He was 48 years old when the Canada Act was passed in 1982. Aubrey was 84 years old when he passed away in 2018.

JOSEPH HAMBURGER[9]

J oseph was born in 1960.
He was 22 years old when the Canada Act was passed in 1982.
Joseph was 47 years old when he passed away in 2007.

SOPHIE HAMBURGER[10]

Sophie was born in 1922.

She was 12 years old when the Dionne Quintuplets were born in 1934.

Sophie was 60 years old when the Canada Act was passed in 1982.

She was 88 years old when she passed away in 2010.

ARTHUR INTRATOR[11]

Arthur was born on April 17, 1926.

He was eight years old when the Dionne Quintuplets were born in 1934.

Arthur was 51 years old when he passed away in 1977.

HOWARD BARRY INTRATOR[12]

Howard was born on July 5, 1961.
He was 16 years old when his father passed away in 1977.
Howard was 21 years old when the Canada Act was passed in 1982.
He was 39 years old when he passed away in 2000.

RITA (TURK) INTRATOR[13]

Rita was born in 1929.

She was five years old when the Dionne Quintuplets were born in 1934.

Rita was 35 years old when her son, Howard Barry, was born in 1961.

She was 48 years old when her husband passed away in 1977.

Rita was 53 years old when the Canada Act was passed in 1982.

She was 71 years old when her son, Howard, passed away in 2000.

Rita was 85 years old when she passed away in 2014.

AARON S. KIZELL[14]

Aaron was born in 1919.

He was 14 years old when the Dionne Quintuplets were born in 1934.

Aaron was 50 years old when his father passed away in 1969.

He was 62 years old when the Canada Act was passed in 1982.

Aaron was 64 years old when his wife passed away in 1984.

He was 67 years old when he passed away in 1987.

BIRDIE RAE (CRAMER) KIZELL[15]

Birdie was born in 1926.

She was eight years old when the Dionne Quintuplets were born in 1834.

Birdie was 56 years old when the Canada Act was passed in 1982.

She was 58 years old when she passed away on February 5, 1984.

JOAN RITA (COWAN) KIZELL[16]

Joan was born in 1933.

She was a year old when the Dionnne Quintuplets were born in 1934.

Joan was 49 years old when the Canada Act was passed in 1982.

She was 56 years old when her father passed away in 1989.

Joan was 69 years old when her mother passed away in 2002.

She was 70 years old when her husband, Raymond Harold Kizell, passed away in 2003.

Joan was 77 years old when she passed away on March 8, 2010.

RAYMOND HAROLD "RAY" KIZELL[17]

Ray was born on January 26, 1924.

He was nine years old when the Dionne Quintuplets were born in 1934.

Ray was 45 years old when his father passed away in 1969.

He was 57 years old when his sister, Doris, passed away in 1996.

Ray was 79 years old when he passed away on May 31, 2003.

LOUIS LANGBORT[18]

Louis was born in 1882.

He was a year old when the mining boom in northern Ontario began in 1883.

Louis was 24 years old when Ontario Hydro was established in 1906.

He was 51 years old when he passed away in 1933.

ANNIE LONGBORT[19]

Annie passed away on May 28, 1942.

ESTHER LONGBORT[20]

E sther passed away on March 7, 1943.

DR. SAMUEL LUDWIN[21]

Samuel was born in Johannesburg, South Africa, on October 16, 1944.

He was 75 years old when he passed away on January 21, 2020.

ELLA MARCUS[22]

Ella was born on June 5, 1919.

She was 14 years old when the Dionne Quintuplets were born in 1834.

Ella was 62 years old when the Canada Act was passed in 1982.

She was 63 years old when she passed away on January 12, 1983.

LEAH (URTICK) MARCUS[23]

Leah was born in Romania in 1897.

She was nine years old when Ontario Hydro was established in 1906.

Leah was 37 years old when the Dionne Quintuplets were born in 1934.

She was 44 years old when she passed away on July 28, 1941.

MORDECHAI "MAX" MARCUS[24]

Max was born in Romania on August 16, 1898.

He was 14 years old when Romania entered into the Second Balkan war in 1913.

Max was 34 years old when the Dionne Quintuplets were born in 1934.

He was 42 years old when his wife passed away in 1941.

Max was 82 years old when he passed away on December 27, 1980.

SAMUEL DAVID MARCUS[25]

Samuel was born September 18, 1925.

He was eight years old when the Dionne Quintuplets were born in 1934.

Samuel was 15 years old when his mother passed away in 1941.

He was 49 years old when he passed away on January 30, 1975.

SIDNEY HARRY ROUTBARD[26]

Sidney was born in 1922.

He was 12 years old when the Dionne Quintuplets were born in 1934.

Sidney was 60 years old when the Canada Act was passed in 1982.

He was 67 years old when he passed away in 1989.

BRONISLAWA RYCZKE[27]

B ronislawa was born in Kolo, Poland in 1912.
She was 22 years old when the Dionne Quintuplets were born in 1934.

Bronislawa was 42 years old when she passed away in 1954.

UNKNOWN SAMUELS[28]

They were born in 1880 and passed away in 1927.

DOROTHY (TEVAN) SHANAS[29]

Dorothy was born in 1925.

She was nine years old when the Dionne Quintuplets were born in 1934.

Dorothy was 57 years old when the Canada Act was passed in 1982.

She was 90 years old when she passed away in 2015.

SAUL SHANUS[30]

S aul was born in 1922.

He was 12 years old when the Dionne Quintuplets were born in 1934.

Saul was 56 years old when he passed away in 1978.

FRANK SHIPARO[31]

Frank was born on March 8, 1951.

He was 30 years old when the Canada Act was passed in 1982.

Frank was 66 years old when he passed away on October 6, 2017.

ESTELLE SILVERMAN[32]

E stelle was born in 1937.
   She was 45 years old when the Canada Act was passed in 1934.
Estella was 64 years old when she passed away in 2001.

JULIUS MOSES SUGARMAN[33]

Julius was born in 1925.

He was nine years old when the Dionne Quintuplets were born in 1934.

Julius was 56 years old when he passed away in 1981.

GERALD JACOB JOSEPH "JERRY" TULCHINSKY[34]

Jerry was born in Brantford, Ontario on September 9, 1933.

He was 48 years old when the Canada Act was passed in 1982.

Jerry was 84 years old when he passed away in Kingston, Ontario on December 13, 2017.

RUTH (RICE) TULCHINSKY[35]

Ruth was born in Lindsay, Ontario on October 18, 1939. She was 42 years old when the Canada Act was passed in 1982. Ruth was 78 years old when her husband, Jerry, passed away in 2017. She was 82 years old when she passed away on April 17, 2022.

ARTHUR DAVID WALFORD[36]

Arthur was a flying officer.

He was killed in an accident in Westbrook, Ontario on February 2, 1943.

Arthur is buried in Kingston, Ontario.

BETH ISRAEL CEMETERY IN BERLIN, NEW HAMPSHIRE, USA

HARRY ABRAMSON[37]

Harry was born in 1920.

He was nine years old when the Great Depression began in 1929.

Harry was 81 years old when he passed away in 2001.

HYMAN ABRAMSON[38]

Hyman was born in Poland in 1885.

He was 14 years old when he immigrated to the USA in 1899.

Hyman was 32 years old when his son, Samuel Gordon, was born in 1917.

He was 35 years old when his son, Harry, was born in 1920.

Hyman ws 44 years old when the Great Depression began in 1929.

He was 90 years old when he passed away in 1975.

IDA ABRAMSON[39]

Ida was born in Russia in 1895.

She was 14 years old when she immigrated to the USA in 1909.

Ida was 15 years old when the Mann Act was passed in 1910.

She was 22 years old when her son, Samuel Gordon, was born in 1917.

Ida was 25 years old when her son, Harry, was born in 1920.

She was 27 years old when her daughter, Alma, was born in 1922.

Ida was 54 years old when NATO was established in 1949.

She was 80 years old when her husband passed away in 1975.

Ida was 84 years old when she passed away in 1979.

MORRIS ADDLESON[40]

Morris was born in Russia in 1868.

He was 17 years old when he immigrated to the USA in 1885.

Morris was 20 years old when the Women's Suffrage movement began in 1890.

He was 28 years old when his son, Harold, was born in 1896.

Morris was 32 years old when the first US navy submarine was constructed in 1900.

He was 36 years old when his daughter, Mina, was born in 1904.

Morris was 40 years old when his daughter, Fanny, was born in 1908.

He was 42 years old when the Mann Act was passed in 1910.

Morris was 59 years old when he passed away in Brooklyn, New York, on October 24, 1927. He is buried in Berlin, New Hampshire.

NELLIE (GREEN) ADDLESON[41]

Nellie was born in Russia in 1868.

She was 19 years old when she immigrated to the USA in 1887.

Nellie was 22 years old when the Women's Suffrage movement began in 1890.

She was 28 years old when her son, Harold, was born in 1896.

Nellie was 36 years old when her daughter, Mina, was born in 1904.

She was 40 years old when her daughter, Fanny, was born in 1908.

Nellie was 42 years old when the Mann Act was passed in 1910.

She was 59 years old when her husband passed away in 1927.

Nellie was 64 years old when she passed away on October 19, 1932.

DAVID COHEN[42]

David was born in Exeter, New Hampshire on May 31, 1899.
He was 17 years old when the US entered WWI in 1917.
David was working as a mechanic when he was drafted into the military.
He was tall, of medium build, with blue eyes and brown hair.

David was 39 years old when he married Marion in Lancaster, New Hampshire on February 11, 1939.

He was 67 years old when he passed away in Lancaster, New Hampshire on May 5, 1967. David is buried in Berlin, New Hampshire.

DANIEL DANNEMAN[43]

Daniel was born in Latvia in 1881.

He was 24 years old when he immigrated to Ellis Island on July 30, 1905.

Daniel was 28 years old when the Mann Act was passed in 1910.

He was 32 years old when he married Bessie in Berlin, New Hampshire on February 18, 1913.

Daniel was 32 years old when his son, Norman, was born in 1914.

He was 35 years old when he was drafted into WWI in 1917. Daniel was working as a watchmaker at the time. He was tall with a medium build, brown hair and brown eyes.

Daniel was 47 years old when the Great Depression began in 1929.

He was 65 years old when the CIA was established in 1947. Daniel passed away on December 3rd.

HARRIET DANNEMAN[44]

Harriet was born in Berlin, New Hampshire on May 1, 1919.

She was 15 years old when the FBI was established in 1935.

Harriet was 27 years old when the CIA was established in 1947. Her father passed away on December 3rd.

She was 47 years old when her mother passed away in 1967.

Harriet was 81 years old when her brother, Norman, passed away in 2000.

She was 90 years old when she passed away in West Stewartstown, New Hampshire on February 7, 2010.

FREDA (LEVIN) DAVIS[45]

Freda was born in 1902.
She was 89 years old when she passed away in 1991.

LEONARD H. DAVIS[46]

Leonard was born on February 28, 1928.

He was two years old when the Star-Spangled Banner was adopted as the national anthem in 1931.

Leonard was six years old when the FBI was established in 1935.

He was 52 years old when he passed away in February 1981.

BESSIE FINKLE[47]

B essie was born in Boston, Massachusetts on September 1, 1899
She was 10 years old when the Mann Act was passed in 1910.

Bessie was 21 years old when she passed away in Berlin, New Hampshire on October 13, 1920.

BENJAMIN GERRISH HOOS[48]

Benjamin was born in the Russian Empire in 1903.

He was a year old when the Russo-Japanese War ended in 1904.

Benjamin was 26 years old when the Great Depression began in 1929.

He was 29 years old when his son, Robert David, was born in 1932.

Benjamin was 32 years old when his daughter, Julia, was born in 1935.

He was 34 years old when the Neutrality Act was passed in 1937.

Benjamin was 81 years old when he passed away on March 5, 1984.

CHARLES ISAACSON[49]

Charles was born in Russia on April 22, 1895.
He was 21 years old when he was drafted into WWI in 1917.
Charles was 88 years old when he passed away on February 2, 1984.

NATHAN PHILIP ISRAELSON[50]

Nathan served in WWI. He was of medium height and build with brown hair and brown eyes. He was from Germany.
He passed away on November 20, 1939.

PHILIP MOSES ISRAELSON[51]

Philip was born in Milan, New Hampshire on August 20, 1887. He was 24 years old when the Girl Scouts were formed in 1912. Philip was 29 years old when he was drafted into WWI. He was tall with a medium build. Philip had brown eyes and black hair. Philip had previously been a sargeant according to his draft papers.

He was 67 years old when he passed away in Rumford, Maine on November 23, 1954. Philip is buried in Berlin, New Hampshire.

ISAAC F. JACOBS[52]

Isaac was born in Germany on April 10, 1837.

He was 43 years old when he married Julia in Manhattan, New York on October 19, 1881.

Isaac was 44 years old when his daughter, Clara, was born in 1882.

He was 46 years old when his son, Fred, was born in 1885.

Isaac was 47 years old when the Statue of Liberty was dedicated in 1886.

He was 48 years old when his daughter, Miriam, was born in 1887.

Isaac was 51 years old when his son, Norman, was born in 1889.

He was 53 years old when his son, Milton, was born in 1891.

Issac was 57 years old when his son, Bernhard Waterman, was born in 1895.

He was 86 years old when he passed away on July 25, 1924.

JULIA (WASSERMANN) JACOBS[53]

Julia was born in Germany on February 22, 1852.

She was 29 years old when she married Isaac Jacobs in Manhattan, New York on October 19, 1881.

Julia was 29 years old when the Chinese Exclusion Act was passed in 1882.

She was 30 years old when her daughter, Clara, was born in 1882.

Julia was 32 years old when her son, Fred, was born in 1885.

She was 33 years old when the Statue of Liberty was dedicated in 1886.

Julia was 35 years old when her daughter, Miriam, was born in 1887.

She was 37 years old when her son, Norman, was born in 1889.

Julia was 39 years old when her son, Milton, was born in 1891.

She was 43 years old when her son, Bernhard Waterman, was born in 1895.

Julia was 72 years old when her husband passed away in 1924.

She was 80 years old when she passed away on June 5, 1932.

HYMAN C. LEWIS[54]

Hyman was born in 1850.
He was 72 years old when he passed away in 1922.

PVT. ROBERT B. LEWIS[55]

Robert was born on December 15, 1890.
He was 86 years old when he passed away on August 12, 1977.

SARAH (SLONIMSKY) LEWIS[56]

Sarah was born in Russia on September 10, 1865.

She was 20 years old when the Statue of Liberty was dedicated in 1886.

Sarah was 21 years old when her son, Leib, was born in 1887.

She was 23 years old when her son, Victor, was born in 1889.

Sarah was 28 years old when Nicholas II was crowned emperor in 1894. Her daughter, Rose, was born the same year.

Sarah was 33 years old when her daughter, Lippe, was born in 1899.

She was 38 years old when her son, Jone, was born in 1904.

Sarah was 57 years old when her husband passed away in 1923.

She was 84 years old when she passed away in 1949.

[1] https://www.wikitree.com/genealogy/Kizell-Family-Tree-1

[2] https://www.wikitree.com/genealogy/Berofe-Family-Tree-1

[3] https://www.wikitree.com/treewidget/Cohen-6256/6

[4] https://www.wikitree.com/genealogy/Fisher-Family-Tree-19036

[5] https://www.wikitree.com/genealogy/Ginsberg-Family-Tree-207

[6] https://www.wikitree.com/genealogy/Goldstein-Family-Tree-1438

[7] https://www.wikitree.com/genealogy/Goldstein-Family-Tree-1676

[8] https://www.wikitree.com/genealogy/Groll-Family-Tree-105

[9] https://www.wikitree.com/genealogy/Hamburger-Family-Tree-228

[10] https://www.wikitree.com/genealogy/Hamburger-Family-Tree-229

[11] https://www.wikitree.com/genealogy/Intrator-Family-Tree-10

[12] https://www.wikitree.com/genealogy/Intrator-Family-Tree-11

[13] https://www.wikitree.com/genealogy/Turk-Family-Tree-798

[14] https://www.wikitree.com/genealogy/Kizell-Family-Tree-4

[15] https://www.wikitree.com/genealogy/Cramer-Family-Tree-2596

[16] https://www.wikitree.com/genealogy/Cowan-Family-Tree-3599

[17] https://www.wikitree.com/genealogy/Kizell-Family-Tree-5

[18] https://www.wikitree.com/genealogy/Langbort-Family-Tree-1

[19] https://www.wikitree.com/genealogy/Longbort-Family-Tree-1

[20] https://www.wikitree.com/genealogy/Longbort-Family-Tree-2

[21] https://www.wikitree.com/genealogy/Ludwin-Family-Tree-7

[22] https://www.wikitree.com/genealogy/Marcus-Family-Tree-662

[23] https://www.wikitree.com/genealogy/Urtick-Family-Tree-1

[24] https://www.wikitree.com/genealogy/Marcus-Family-Tree-663

[25] https://www.wikitree.com/genealogy/Marcus-Family-Tree-664

[26] https://www.wikitree.com/genealogy/Routbard-Family-Tree-1

[27] https://www.wikitree.com/genealogy/Ryczke-Family-Tree-4

[28] https://www.wikitree.com/genealogy/Samuels-Family-Tree-1150

[29] https://www.wikitree.com/genealogy/Tevan-Family-Tree-1

[30] https://www.wikitree.com/genealogy/Shanas-Family-Tree-2

[31] https://www.wikitree.com/genealogy/Shiparo-Family-Tree-2

[32] https://www.wikitree.com/genealogy/Silverman-Family-Tree-607

[33] https://www.wikitree.com/genealogy/Sugarman-Family-Tree-71

[34] https://www.wikitree.com/genealogy/Tulchinsky-Family-Tree-2

[35] https://www.wikitree.com/genealogy/Rice-Family-Tree-21264

[36] https://www.wikitree.beth/genealogy/Walford-Family-Tree-365

[37] https://www.wikitree.com/genealogy/Abramson-Family-Tree-255

[38] https://www.wikitree.com/genealogy/Abramson-Family-Tree-256

[39] https://www.wikitree.com/genealogy/Unknown-Family-Tree-625011

[40] https://www.wikitree.com/genealogy/Addelson-Family-Tree-1

[41] https://www.wikitree.com/genealogy/Green-Family-Tree-50511

[42] https://www.wikitree.com/genealogy/Cohen-Family-Tree-6257

[43] https://www.wikitree.com/genealogy/Danneman-Family-Tree-13

[44] https://www.wikitree.com/genealogy/Danneman-Family-Tree-14

[45] https://www.wikitree.com/genealogy/Levin-Family-Tree-958

[46] https://www.wikitree.com/genealogy/Davis-Family-Tree-102998

[47] https://www.wikitree.com/genealogy/Finkle-Family-Tree-242

[48] https://www.wikitree.com/genealogy/Hoos-Family-Tree-98

[49] https://www.wikitree.com/genealogy/Isaacson-Family-Tree-485

[50] https://www.wikitree.com/genealogy/Israelson-Family-Tree-35

[51] https://www.wikitree.com/genealogy/Israelson-Family-Tree-36

[52] https://www.wikitree.com/genealogy/Jacobs-Family-Tree-16617

[53] https://www.wikitree.com/genealogy/Wassermann-Family-Tree-40

[54] https://www.wikitree.com/genealogy/Lewis-Family-Tree-54369

[55] https://www.wikitree.com/genealogy/Lewis-Family-Tree-54370

[56] https://www.wikitree.com/genealogy/Slonimsky-Family-Tree-11

Don't miss out!

Visit the website below and you can sign up to receive emails whenever Angeline Gallant publishes a new book. There's no charge and no obligation.

https://books2read.com/r/B-A-QGSI-CAVCC

Also by Angeline Gallant

A Dragon's Diary
Dreaming of Dragons

Calling Her Heart
Whisper of the Heart
No Turning Back
Forsake Me Not
Hear My Cry
Calling Her Heart Boxed Set Volumes 1-4

FORGET ME NOT
Victoria, Ontario's Babies 1894 - 1895

Keeper Of Secrets
A Lady's Secret

Midnight's Awakening

Heart of the Storm
Walking Through The Storm
Midnight's Awakening boxed set volumes 1-3

Secrets of the Underworld
Deklan's Dragons
Secrets of the Underworld Volumes 1 & 2

Tell My Story Collection
Tell My Story: England 1852

The Grave Whisperer
Wedding Bells in Kingston, Ontario, Canada 1923
St. Paul's Anglican Churchyard Kingston, Ontario, Canada A-B
St. Paul's Anglican Churchyard, Kingston, Ontario, Canada C - D
St. Paul's Anglican Churchyard, Kingston, Ontario, Canada G - H
St. Paul's Anglican Churchyard, Kingston, Ontario, Canada J - N
St. Paul's Anglican Churchyard, Kingston, Ontario, Canada O - R
St. Paul's Anglican Churchyard, Kingston, Ontario, Canada S - T
St. Paul's Anglican Churchyard, Kingston, Ontario T - Z
Small Graveyards & Burial Grounds: Kingston, Ontario, Canada
Cataraqui United Church Cemetery 1
Cataraqui United Church Cemetery 2
Cataraqui United Church Cemetary 3
Cataraqui United Church Cemetery 4
Cataraqui United Church Cemetery 5
Beth Israel Cemetery

The Wolf Whisperer Series
The Cry of the Wolf
Captured Heart
Journey of the Heart
Fate's Legacy
Wolf Whisperer volumes 1 & 2
Endless White
The Wolf Whisperer Volumes 1-4

Standalone
Winds of Change vol 1-3

Watch for more at https://www.goodreads.com/author/show/19703964.Angeline_Gallant.

9 798215 768952